Morning Greeting Words of Encouragements:

Morning Greeting Words of Encouragements:

Forever Book Calendar

Randy Parson

© 2017 Randy Parson
All rights reserved.

ISBN: 1546832734
ISBN 13: 9781546832737

Dedication

*I DEDICATE THIS BOOK IN MEMORY
OF MY MOTHER LOU W. PARSON,
THE SWEETEST SOUL I KNOW.*

*ALSO, I DEDICATE THIS BOOK TO MY
DAUGHTER MARANDA, MY SISTERS ANITA
AND JANET, AND ALL MY NIECES AND
NEPHEWS AND BROTHER-IN-LAWS.*

*TO MY COUSIN JAMES JOHNSON JR. (BOO) AND
OUR FAVORITE SIGN-OFF - HALLA-HALLA-HALLA.*

Disclaimer

I AM CONFIDENT THAT OVER 98% OF THE 'MORNING GREETING WORDS OF ENCOURAGEMENTS ARE MY ORIGINAL CONCEPTION AND PHRASEOLOGY.

HOWEVER, EVERY ATTEMPT HAS BEEN MADE TO CREDIT STATEMENTS FROM THE HOLY BIBLE WHERE USED AND FROM OTHER KNOWN ORIGINS. ADDITIONALLY, I USED QUOTATION MARKS AROUND PHRASES IN WHICH THE ORIGINATOR IS UNKNOWN.

THE PICTURE ON THE COVER IS THE SOLE PROPERTY OF THE AUTHOR AND ANY REPRODUCTION OR RE-PRINTING OF THIS PICTURE MAY BE DONE ONLY WITH THE AUTHOR'S PERMISSION.

Foreword

These "Morning Greeting Words of Encouragements" are a compilation of what I sent primarily to my Daughter MaRanda for approximately three-years.

I also shared many of the greetings with others such as, TOD-Family (i.e., TheObamaDiary.com) and siblings Gloria and George from Cincinnati, whom I met on Amtrak's California Zephyr train to San Francisco in 2016.

*Note: The first day of each month starts with the same "Morning Greeting Words of Encouragements".

I hope you Benefit Tremendously from these Greeting Words of Encouragements, as well as share them with family and friends.

January
Day 1

Good morning, I hope all is well with you this lovely New Years morning. I hope that God's grace, loving-kindness, and mercy is bestowed upon you today.

Reflective Thoughts:
_____
_____
_____

January
Day 2

Good morning, I hope all is well with you this lovely morning. I hope that you demonstrate a confident, optimistic, and positive outlook today.

Reflective Thoughts:
_____
_____
_____

January
Day 3

Good morning, I hope all is well with you this lovely morning. I hope that glorious praise, honor, and distinction Are bestowed upon you today.

Reflective Thoughts:

_____
_____
_____

January
Day 4

Good morning, I hope all is well with you this lovely morning. I hope you display a strong vigorous, zealous, and enlivened countenance today.

Reflective Thoughts:

_____
_____
_____

January
Day 5

Good morning, I hope all is well with you this lovely morning. I hope you don't hesitate to give thanks to whom it's due, give an encouraging smile to one with the pensive look, and provide hugs to those in need today.

Reflective Thoughts:

___
___
___

January
Day 6

Good morning, I hope all is well with you this lovely morning. I hope you have a wonderful adventurous, enterprising, and innovative day today.

Reflective Thoughts:
_____
_____
_____

January
Day 7

Good morning, I hope all is well with you this lovely morning. I hope you have a gleeful, exuberant, and jovial time today.

Reflective Thoughts:

_____
_____
_____

January
Day 8

Good morning, I hope all is well with you this lovely morning. Don't be afraid to step out of your comfort zone to assist others, to swallow your pride in order to acknowledge your mistakes, and to share your blessings with others today.

Reflective Thoughts:
___
___
___

January
Day 9

Good morning, I hope all is well with you this lovely morning. I hope you have an astounding, magical, and stunningly-surprising fun-loving day today.

Reflective Thoughts:
_____
_____
_____

January
Day 10

Good morning, I hope all is well with you this lovely morning. I hope that your attitude is exemplary, illustrative, and quintessential of goodness today.

Reflective Thoughts:
_____
_____
_____

January
Day 11

Good morning, I hope all is well with you this lovely morning. I hope that God grants you all your needs, wants, and desires today.

Reflective Thoughts:

_____
_____
_____

January
Day 12

Good morning, I hope all is well with you this lovely morning. I hope your day is filled with admiration, appreciation, and reverence of The Almighty today.

Reflective Thoughts:
_____
_____
_____

January
Day 13

Good morning, I hope all is well with you this lovely morning. I hope you are blessed with good-fortune, good-health, and a good-time today.

Reflective Thoughts:

_____
_____
_____

January
Day 14

Good morning, I hope all is well with you this lovely morning. I hope you display an inexhaustible, indefatigable, and pertinacious desire to attain your visions today.

Reflective Thoughts:
___
___
___

January
Day 15

Good morning, I hope all is well with you this lovely morning. I hope that the kindness you show others is evergreen, never-ending, and enduring today.

Reflective Thoughts:

_____
_____
_____

January
Day 16

Good morning, I hope all is well with you this lovely morning. I hope you exercise serenity today to accept the things you don't need to change, change the things you do need to change, and to know the difference between the two. – Modified Serenity Prayer-

Reflective Thoughts:

_____
_____
_____

January
Day 17

Good morning, I hope all is well with you this lovely morning. I hope you are confident, encouraged, and optimistic about what you're going to achieve today.

Reflective Thoughts:

_____
_____
_____

January
Day 18

Good morning, I hope all is well with you this lovely morning. Do know, the more that you work at maintaining your integrity, goodness, and principled character, it becomes habitual each today.

Reflective Thoughts:

January
Day 19

Good morning, I hope all is well with you this lovely morning. I hope you wear your enchanting, endearing, and delectable smile today.

Reflective Thoughts:
_____
_____
_____

January
Day 20

Good morning, I hope all is well with you this lovely morning. I hope you have a no-holds-barred, undeniably, positively, jolly-good-time today.

Reflective Thoughts:

_____
_____
_____

January
Day 21

Good morning, I hope all is well with you this lovely morning. I hope that you are energized, motivated, and stimulated to do great things today.

Reflective Thoughts:
_____
_____
_____

January
Day 22

Good morning, I hope all is well with you this lovely morning. I hope you have one of the most wonderfully-gratifying, super-sensational, and stupendously-crackerjack day today.

Reflective Thoughts:

_____
_____
_____

January
Day 23

Good morning, I hope all is well with you this lovely morning. I hope you attain the dandiest, finest, and loveliest things in your life today.

Reflective Thoughts:
_____
_____
_____

January
Day 24

Good morning, I hope all is well with you this lovely morning. I hope you develop a dare-deviling, entrepreneurial, and pioneering attitude today.

Reflective Thoughts:
_____
_____
_____

January
Day 25

Good morning, I hope all is well with you this lovely morning. I hope your affable, congenial, and simpatico persona is on full display today.

Reflective Thoughts:

_____
_____
_____

January
Day 26

Good morning, I hope all is well with you this lovely morning. I hope you're able to turn any negative situation into a positive, problems into opportunities, and challenges into great ideas today.

Reflective Thoughts:
___
___
___

January
Day 27

Good morning, I hope all is well with you this lovely morning. I hope you display your sunny, energetic, and suave disposition today.

Reflective Thoughts:

___
___
___

January
Day 28

Good morning, I hope all is well with you this lovely morning. I hope you enjoy good-humor, side-splitting, and off-the-chain laughter today.

Reflective Thoughts:
_____
_____
_____

January
Day 29

Good morning, I hope all is well with you this lovely morning. I hope you use your vessel full of understanding, your wealth of knowledge, and your vast experience to successfully face all your challenges today.

Reflective Thoughts:
_____
_____
_____

January
Day 30

Good morning, I hope all is well with you this lovely morning. I hope your imagination take you to places you want to be, expose you to the things you desire, and provide the answers to all that you seek today.

Reflective Thoughts:

_____
_____
_____

January
Day 31

Good morning, I hope all is well with you this lovely morning. I hope you experiences unique, unparalleled, and transcendental favorable moments today.

Reflective Thoughts:
___
___
___

February
Day 1

Good morning, I hope all is well with you this lovely morning. I hope that God's grace, loving-kindness, and mercy is bestowed upon you today.

Reflective Thoughts:
_____
_____
_____

February
Day 2

Good morning, I hope all is well with you this lovely morning. I hope you have a fresh, energetic, and zippy day today.

Reflective Thoughts:

_____
_____
_____

February
Day 3

Good morning, I hope all is well with you this lovely morning. I hope you have a very gratifying, productive, and rewarding day today.

Reflective Thoughts:

_____
_____
_____

February
Day 4

Good morning, I hope all is well with you this lovely morning. I hope your caring, compassionate, and considerate persona is on full display today.

Reflective Thoughts:
_____
_____
_____

February
Day 5

Good morning, I hope all is well with you this lovely morning. I hope you desire to show your elegance, social grace, and sophistication today.

Reflective Thoughts:

_____
_____
_____

February
Day 6

Good morning, I hope all is well with you this lovely morning. I hope you have a foot-stomping, heart-throbbing, jolly good time today.

Reflective Thoughts:
_____
_____
_____

February
Day 7

Good morning, I hope all is well with you this lovely morning. I hope you have a care-free, easygoing, and laid-back day today.

Reflective Thoughts:
_____
_____
_____

February
Day 8

Good morning, I hope all is well with you this lovely morning. I hope that when you see someone surprisingly-joyfully-tearful, you're able to shed a tear; when you see someone crying laughing, you're able to cry with laughter; and when you see someone scream with happiness, you're able to gush-forth a scream with happiness today.

Reflective Thoughts:
___
___
___

February
Day 9

Good morning, I hope all is well with you this lovely morning. I hope that your heart, soul, and mind are energized today to do great things.

Reflective Thoughts:
___
___
___

February
Day 10

Good morning, I hope all is well with you this lovely morning. I hope that you are filled with knowledge, understanding, and wisdom in all things you encounter today.

Reflective Thoughts:

_____
_____
_____

February
Day 11

Good morning, I hope all is well with you this lovely morning. I hope that you are filled with adventure, excitement, and great joy today.

Reflective Thoughts:
_____
_____
_____

February
Day 12

Good morning, I hope all is well with you this lovely morning. I hope that you have a spirit of caring, giving, and uplifting toward others today.

Reflective Thoughts:

_____
_____
_____

February
Day 13

Good morning, I hope all is well with you this lovely morning. I hope that you have a festively joyous, jubilant, and upbeat day today.

Reflective Thoughts:
_____
_____
_____

February
Day 14

Good morning, I hope all is well with you this lovely morning. I hope that you acquire, achieve, and obtain all that you desire today.

Reflective Thoughts:
_____
_____
_____

February
Day 15

Good morning, I hope all is well with you this lovely morning. I hope that you are able to recognize and receive; good advice, wise counsel, and providential-forethought today.

Reflective Thoughts:

February
Day 16

Good morning, I hope all is well with you this lovely morning. I hope that all your needs, wants, and likes are granted to you today.

Reflective Thoughts:

_____
_____
_____

February
Day 17

Good morning, I hope all is well with you this lovely morning. I hope you have a really cool, nifty, and terrific day today.

Reflective Thoughts:
_____
_____
_____

February
Day 18

Good morning, I hope all is well with you this lovely morning. I hope that your performance is exemplary, first-rate, and superb today.

Reflective Thoughts:
___
___
___

February
Day 19

Good morning, I hope all is well with you this lovely morning. I hope that you vicariously live, in the ultimate home, work in that ultimate position and take that ultimate vacation today. So, when it happens, it will be like déjà vu.

Reflective Thoughts:
___
___
___

February
Day 20

Good morning, I hope all is well with you this lovely morning. I hope that you have a cheery, delightful, and gleeful day today.

Reflective Thoughts:
___
___
___

February
Day 21

Good morning, I hope all is well with you this lovely morning. I hope that your courteous, debonair, and pleasant persona is on full display today.

Reflective Thoughts:

_____
_____
_____

February
Day 22

Good morning, I hope all is well with you this lovely morning. I hope that while facing all your challenges and obstacles, you remain calm, cool, and collected today.

Reflective Thoughts:
___
___
___

February
Day 23

Good morning, I hope all is well with you this lovely morning. I hope that you are enthusiastic, excited, and stimulated by the start of this new day today.

Reflective Thoughts:
_____
_____
_____

February
Day 24

Good morning, I hope all is well with you this lovely morning. I hope that your craving for happiness, your longing for joy, and your yearning for a good-time is fulfilled today.

Reflective Thoughts:
_____
_____
_____

February
Day 25

Good morning, I hope all is well with you this lovely morning. I hope that your eyes see, your ears hear, and you mind conceive all the goodness God has prepared for you today.

Reflective Thoughts:

_____
_____
_____

February
Day 26

Good morning, I hope all is well with you this lovely morning. I hope that you grace yourself with your courteous, humble, and thoughtful disposition today.

Reflective Thoughts:

_____
_____
_____

February
Day 27

Good morning, I hope all is well with you this lovely morning. I hope that the start of your day is as fresh as an ocean morning breeze, as serene as a clear blue sky, and as delightful as an early morning smile today.

Reflective Thoughts:
___
___
___

February
Day 28

Good morning, I hope all is well with you this lovely morning. Don't be afraid to step out of your comfort zone to assist others, to swallow your pride in order to acknowledge your mistakes, and to share your blessings with others today.

Reflective Thoughts:
___
___
___

February
Day 29

Good morning, I hope all is well with you this lovely morning. I hope you have a day filled with exciting anticipation, gleeful with great expectation, and steeped in fun-filled preparation for all the good that comes your way today.

Reflective Thoughts:

_____
_____
_____

March
Day 1

Good morning, I hope all is well with you this lovely morning. I hope that God's grace, loving-kindness, and mercy is bestowed upon you today.

Reflective Thoughts:
_____
_____
_____

March
Day 2

Good morning, I hope all is well with you this lovely morning. I hope you wear your charitable, hospitable, and munificent disposition today.

Reflective Thoughts:
_____
_____
_____

March
Day 3

Good morning, I hope all is well with you this lovely morning. I hope that you elevate, honor, and reward others today.

Reflective Thoughts:
_____
_____
_____

March
Day 4

Good morning, I hope all is well with you this lovely morning. I hope that your captivating, fascinating, mesmerizing persona is on full display today.

Reflective Thoughts:
___
___
___

March
Day 5

Good morning, I hope all is well with you this lovely morning. I hope that you acquire, effectuate, and obtain all your desires and goals today.

Reflective Thoughts:

_____
_____
_____

March
Day 6

Good morning, I hope all is well with you this lovely morning. I hope that you are able to do the things that brings you contentment, enjoyment, and happiness today.

Reflective Thoughts:

_____
_____
_____

March
Day 7

Good morning, I hope all is well with you this lovely morning. I hope that you have a mellow, smooth, and tranquil day today.

Reflective Thoughts:

_____
_____
_____

March
Day 8

Good morning, I hope all is well with you this lovely morning. I hope whenever you face controversy, you walk with your head high, stride like royalty, and toast with grace today.

Reflective Thoughts:
_____
_____
_____

March
Day 9

Good morning, I hope all is well with you this lovely morning. I hope you have a delightful, fascinating, and pleasant day today.

Reflective Thoughts:
___
___
___

March
Day 10

Good morning, I hope all is well with you this lovely morning. I hope that you are granted favor, good-will, and obligement from all whom you encounter today.

Reflective Thoughts:
___
___
___

March
Day 11

Good morning, I hope all is well with you this lovely morning. I hope that you are guarded, protected, and secure in all things you do today.

Reflective Thoughts:
_____
_____
_____

March
Day 12

Good morning, I hope all is well with you this lovely morning. I hope that your affable, cordial, and suave persona is full display today.

Reflective Thoughts:

_____
_____
_____

March
Day 13

Good morning, I hope all is well with you this lovely morning. I hope you let your actions bring about good rather than good causing you to act, let your smile change the world rather than the world change your smile, and let your faith increase your hope rather than like-of-faith causing you to loose hope today.

Reflective Thoughts:
___
___
___

March
Day 14

Good morning, I hope all is well with you this lovely morning. I hope you clothe yourself in empathy and empathize with others, dress yourself in vicariousness and live vicariously in others, and adorn yourself in sympathy and be sympathetic toward others today.

Reflective Thoughts:
___
___
___

March
Day 15

Good morning, I hope all is well with you this lovely morning. I hope that you strive to be as dependable as water will be wet, as reliable as the sun will be hot and as resourceful as a concierge today.

Reflective Thoughts:

_____
_____
_____

March
Day 16

Good morning, I hope all is well with you this lovely morning. I hope that your effervescent, spirited, and vivacious persona is on full display today.

Reflective Thoughts:
___
___
___

March
Day 17

Good morning, I hope all is well with you this lovely morning. I hope you are mindful that God has given you a mind to understand complexities, gain as much knowledge as you seek, and to see your visions today.

Reflective Thoughts:
_____
_____
_____

March
Day 18

Good morning, I hope all is well with you this lovely morning. I hope your admirable, first-rate, and outstanding character is on full display today.

Reflective Thoughts:
_____
_____
_____

March
Day 19

Good morning, I hope all is well with you this lovely morning. I hope you have a one-of-a-kind, incomparable, and an unmatched exciting day today.

Reflective Thoughts:

___
___
___

March
Day 20

Good morning, I hope all is well with you this lovely morning. I hope you have an amazing, breath-taking, and mind-blowing delightful day today.

Reflective Thoughts:
_____
_____
_____

March
Day 21

Good morning, I hope all is well with you this lovely morning. I hope you have a transcendental, unique, and an unparalleled wonderful experience today.

Reflective Thoughts:
_____
_____
_____

March
Day 22

Good morning, I hope all is well with you this lovely morning. I hope you take a moment to sip your favorite drink, prop your legs up, lean back with head in hands, close your eyes and travel to a wonderful place you've never been; and with a smile on your face, say Halla, Halla, Halla today.

Reflective Thoughts:
_____
_____
_____

March
Day 23

Good morning, I hope all is well with you this lovely morning. I hope you attain your visions, ascend to greatness, and rise to your desired quality of life today.

Reflective Thoughts:
_____
_____
_____

March
Day 24

Good morning, I hope all is well with you this lovely morning. I hope you are met with friendly-reception, generosity, and hospitality from everyone you encounter today.

Reflective Thoughts:

_____
_____
_____

March
Day 25

Good morning, I hope all is well with you this lovely morning. I hope you are clothe in ataraxia, showered calmness, and sprinkled with quietness today.

Reflective Thoughts:
_____
_____
_____

March
Day 26

Good morning, I hope all is well with you this lovely morning. I hope that you display a benevolent, caring, and humanitarian spirit today.

Reflective Thoughts:
___
___
___

March
Day 27

Good morning, I hope all is well with you this lovely morning. I hope you have a silky-smooth, hang-loose, and unconstrained day today.

Reflective Thoughts:

___
___
___

March
Day 28

Good morning, I hope all is well with you this lovely morning. I hope that you meet all of your challenges with certitude, determination, and grit today.

Reflective Thoughts:

_____
_____
_____

March
Day 29

Good morning, I hope all is well with you this lovely morning. I hope that your witty, brilliantly-clever, and vivacious persona is on full display today.

Reflective Thoughts:
___
___
___

March
Day 30

Good morning, I hope all is well with you this lovely morning. I hope you have an amusing, gratifying, and an unforgettable rewarding day today.

Reflective Thoughts:
___
___
___

March
Day 31

Good morning, I hope all is well with you this lovely morning. I hope that you demonstrate a commendable, exemplary, and sterling performance in everything you do today.

Reflective Thoughts:
_____
_____
_____

April
Day 1

Good morning, I hope all is well with you this lovely morning. I hope that God's grace, loving-kindness, and mercy is bestowed upon you today.

Reflective Thoughts:
___
___
___

April
Day 2

Good morning, I hope all is well with you this lovely morning. I hope that throughout the day you're able to find moments of peace when you need it, moments of happiness when you seek it, and moments of joy when you desire it today.

Reflective Thoughts:

___
___
___

April
Day 3

Good morning, I hope all is well with you this lovely morning. I hope all the people you meet today know that your friendship is in perpetuity, your kindness is perpetual, and your love is to eternity.

Reflective Thoughts:

_____
_____
_____

April
Day 4

Good morning, I hope all is well with you this lovely morning. I hope that you are refreshed, rejuvenated, and reinvigorated to pursue your visions today.

Reflective Thoughts:
___
___
___

April
Day 5

Good morning, I hope all is well with you this lovely morning. I hope that you accept, embrace, and receive gladly, opportunities for change today.

Reflective Thoughts:

_____
_____
_____

April
Day 6

Good morning, I hope all is well with you this lovely morning. I hope you display an altruistic, magnanimous, and an unselfish spirit toward others today.

Reflective Thoughts:
___
___
___

April
Day 7

Good morning, I hope all is well with you this lovely morning. I hope you have an easygoing, peaceful, and tranquil day today.

Reflective Thoughts:
___
___
___

April
Day 8

Good morning, I hope all is well with you this lovely morning. I hope all those you encounter, acknowledge you as a breath-of-fresh-air, a force-for-good, and a good-luck-charm today.

Reflective Thoughts:

_____
_____
_____

April
Day 9

Good morning, I hope all is well with you this lovely morning. I hope that you are filled with a spirit of adventure, coolness, and courageousness, today.

Reflective Thoughts:
_____
_____
_____

April
Day 10

Good morning, I hope all is well with you this lovely morning. I hope that you have one of the most productive, rewarding, and an unforgettable day today.

Reflective Thoughts:
_____
_____
_____

April
Day 11

Good morning, I hope all is well with you this lovely morning. I hope that your classy, suave, and Dame persona is on full display today.

Reflective Thoughts:
_____
_____
_____

April
Day 12

Good morning, I hope all is well with you this lovely morning. I hope that you have joyous, magnificent, and superb fantastic day today.

Reflective Thoughts:
_____
_____
_____

April
Day 13

Good morning, I hope all is well with you this lovely morning. I hope that you display a considerate, courteous, and gracious attitude toward others today.

Reflective Thoughts:
___
___
___

April
Day 14

Good morning, I hope all is well with you this lovely morning. I hope you have an amazing, phenomenal, and sensational day today.

Reflective Thoughts:
_____
_____
_____

April
Day 15

Good morning, I hope all is well with you this lovely morning. I hope that your determination to be the best at what you're doing at the very moment you're doing it, is such that you are willing to walk across the desert sands, swim the most expansive ocean, and climb to the top of the highest mountain today.

Reflective Thoughts:
_____
_____
_____

April
Day 16

Good morning, I hope all is well with you this lovely morning. I hope that your greatest character, dynamic personality, and wonderful soul, is on full display today.

Reflective Thoughts:

_____
_____
_____

April
Day 17

Good morning, I hope all is well with you this lovely morning. I hope that you show compassion, kindness, and selflessness, toward everyone you encounter today.

Reflective Thoughts:
___
___
___

April
Day 18

Good morning, I hope all is well with you this lovely morning. I hope that you have a convivial, festive, and merry good time today.

Reflective Thoughts:
___
___
___

April
Day 19

Good morning, I hope all is well with you this lovely morning. I hope that your dynamic, energetic, and vivacious persona is on full display today.

Reflective Thoughts:
___
___
___

April
Day 20

Good morning, I hope all is well with you this lovely morning. I hope that you approach all things with enthusiasm, excitement, and passion today.

Reflective Thoughts:
___
___
___

April
Day 21

Good morning, I hope all is well with you this lovely morning. I hope that you display an approachable, open-minded, and tolerant mind-set today.

Reflective Thoughts:
___
___
___

April
Day 22

Good morning, I hope all is well with you this lovely morning. I hope you display your fascinatingly alluring, engaging, and winsome smile today.

Reflective Thoughts:
___
___
___

April
Day 23

Good morning, I hope all is well with you this lovely morning. I hope that you are given accommodation, consideration, and favor, in all that you pursue today.

Reflective Thoughts:
_____
_____
_____

April
Day 24

Good morning, I hope all is well with you this lovely morning. I hope that you will give your very best at whatever you do, at the very moment you are doing it today.

Reflective Thoughts:

_____
_____
_____

April
Day 25

Good morning, I hope all is well with you this lovely morning. I hope you have a delightful, enjoyable, and jubilant day today.

Reflective Thoughts:

_____
_____
_____

April
Day 26

Good morning, I hope all is well with you this lovely morning. I hope you exchange a wink, offer a hug, and give a that-a-boy to whom it's due today.

Reflective Thoughts:
_____
_____
_____

April
Day 27

Good morning, I hope all is well with you this lovely morning. I hope that throughout the day you're able to find moments of peace when you need it, moments of happiness when you seek it, and moments of joy when you desire it today.

Reflective Thoughts:
___
___
___

April
Day 28

Good morning, I hope all is well with you this lovely morning. I hope your generosity, kindliness, and magnanimity is on full display today.

Reflective Thoughts:
_____
_____
_____

April
Day 29

Good morning, I hope all is well with you this lovely morning. I hope that your countenance is as reflective as a rainbow, look as tender as a dove, and as attentive as an eagle today.

Reflective Thoughts:
_____
_____
_____

April
Day 30

Good morning, I hope all is well with you this lovely morning. I hope you start your day with an optimistic, self-confident, and upbeat disposition today.

Reflective Thoughts:
___
___
___

May
Day 1

Good morning, I hope all is well with you this lovely morning. I hope that God's grace, loving-kindness, and mercy is bestowed upon you today.

Reflective Thoughts:
___
___
___

May
Day 2

Good morning, I hope all is well with you this lovely morning. I hope that your absolute terrific, extremely wonderful, and extraordinarily great persona is on full display today.

Reflective Thoughts:
_____
_____
_____

May
Day 3

Good morning, I hope all is well with you this lovely morning. I hope you have an awesome, mind-blowing, and zero-cool day today.

Reflective Thoughts:
_____
_____
_____

May
Day 4

Good morning, I hope all is well with you this lovely morning. I hope your day is packed with mind-blowing-excitement, heartwarming-surprises, and jaw-dropping-hullabaloos today.

Reflective Thoughts:
___
___
___

May
Day 5

Good morning, I hope all is well with you this lovely morning. I hope you have an enjoyable, entertaining, and pleasurable day today.

Reflective Thoughts:

_____
_____
_____

May
Day 6

Good morning, I hope all is well with you this lovely morning. I hope you are full of laughter, jubilance, and rejoicing today.

Reflective Thoughts:

_____
_____
_____

May
Day 7

Good morning, I hope all is well with you this lovely morning. Let the words from your mouth, the meditation of your heart and the actions you take be authentic, bona fide, and genuine today.

Reflective Thoughts:
___
___
___

May
Day 8

Good morning, I hope all is well with you this lovely morning. I hope that you take measures to prepare for enjoyment, be studious to gain knowledge, and be prayerful to gain wisdom today.

Reflective Thoughts:
___
___
___

May
Day 9

Good morning, I hope all is well with you this lovely morning. Never be afraid to ask for what you need, want, and like. When you ask; ask as though you are going to get it, and have a humbling spirit. Don't accept "no". Stay in the conversation, even complimenting and offering alternatives.

Reflective Thoughts:
___
___
___

May
Day 10

Good morning, I hope all is well with you this lovely morning. I encourage you to be amazing, be dazzling, and be sensational today.

Reflective Thoughts:
___
___
___

May
Day 11

Good morning, I hope all is well with you this lovely morning. I hope you display an appreciative, grateful, and thankful attitude today.

Reflective Thoughts:
___
___
___

May
Day 12

Good morning, I hope all is well with you this lovely morning. I hope all your needs, wants, and likes are granted to you today.

Reflective Thoughts:
___
___
___

May
Day 13

Good morning, I hope all is well with you this lovely morning. I hope that your charming, elegant, and dainty persona is on full display today.

Reflective Thoughts:
___
___
___

May
Day 14

Good morning, I hope all is well with you this lovely morning. I hope you seek to encourage, enliven and inspire those you encounter today.

Reflective Thoughts:
___
___
___

May
Day 15

Good morning, I hope all is well with you this lovely morning. I hope that you never downplay your discernible, perceptible, and intuitive qualities. Trust yourself and maintain your integrity, no matter what. You don't want to be left saying; if I woulda-coulda-shoulda today or any day.

Reflective Thoughts:
___
___
___

May
Day 16

Good morning, I hope all is well with you this lovely morning. I hope that you are equipped with brilliance, inventiveness, and sagacity to accomplish all things today.

Reflective Thoughts:
_____
_____
_____

May
Day 17

Good morning, I hope all is well with you this lovely morning. I hope that you have an optimistic, positive, and upbeat attitude about your future, today.

Reflective Thoughts:
_____
_____
_____

May
Day 18

Good morning, I hope all is well with you this lovely morning. I hope that the display of your charming, effervescent, and cheerful personality brightens up the world today.

Reflective Thoughts:
_____
_____
_____

May
Day 19

Good morning, I hope all is well with you this lovely morning. I hope you can make the sacrifices that are necessary to pursue your desires and visions in order to have the future you want.

Reflective Thoughts:

_____
_____
_____

May
Day 20

Good morning, I hope all is well with you this lovely morning. I hope you have a groovy, hair-raising, and sensational day today.

Reflective Thoughts:
_____
_____
_____

May
Day 21

Good morning, I hope all is well with you this lovely morning. I hope that you encourage, lift-up, and make others laugh with joy today.

Reflective Thoughts:
___
___
___

May
Day 22

Good morning, I hope all is well with you this lovely morning. I hope all that you do is indicative of your warm heart, charming personality, and your electrifying individuality today.

Reflective Thoughts:

_____
_____
_____

May
Day 23

Good morning, I hope all is well with you this lovely morning. I hope you have an enjoyable, peaceful, and reflective day today.

Reflective Thoughts:
_____
_____
_____

May
Day 24

Good morning, I hope all is well with you this lovely morning. I hope you look out for the concerns, needs, and welfare of others today.

Reflective Thoughts:
___
___
___

May
Day 25

Good morning, I hope all is well with you this lovely morning. I hope that your countenance brings cheerfulness, happiness, and joy to all those you encounter today.

Reflective Thoughts:
_____
_____
_____

May
Day 26

Good morning, I hope all is well with you this lovely morning. I hope you have a cool, mellifluous, and relaxing day today.

Reflective Thoughts:
___
___
___

May
Day 27

Good morning, I hope all is well with you this lovely morning. I hope you have a creative, inventive, and productive day today.

Reflective Thoughts:
___
___
___

May
Day 28

Good morning, I hope all is well with you this lovely morning. I hope that you have a glorious, joyous, and superfantastic day today.

Reflective Thoughts:
_____
_____
_____

May
Day 29

Good morning, I hope all is well with you this lovely morning. I hope that you take account of all the wonderful things that has happen to you and embrace your life, congratulate yourself, and do your happy-dance today.

Reflective Thoughts:
_____
_____
_____

May
Day 30

Good morning, I hope all is well with you this lovely morning. I hope you have one of the most exciting, exquisite, and fun-filled day of your life today.

Reflective Thoughts:
_____
_____
_____

May
Day 31

Good morning, I hope all is well with you this lovely morning. I hope that you show empathy, tenderness, and warmth towards others today.

Reflective Thoughts:
___
___
___

June
Day 1

Good morning, I hope all is well with you this lovely morning. I hope that God's grace, loving-kindness, and mercy is bestowed upon you today.

Reflective Thoughts:
_____
_____
_____

June
Day 2

Good morning, I hope all is well with you this lovely morning. I hope you an enjoyable, fun-filled, and pleasant day today.

Reflective Thoughts:
___
___
___

June
Day 3

Good morning, I hope all is well with you this lovely morning. I hope you have a gratifying, pleasant, and an unforgettable rewarding day today.

Reflective Thoughts:

___
___
___

June
Day 4

Good morning, I hope all is well with you this lovely morning. I hope you have a restful, exciting, and productive day today.

Reflective Thoughts:
_____
_____
_____

June
Day 5

Good morning, I hope all is well with you this lovely morning. I hope that you have an insouciant, carefree, and happy-go-lucky day today.

Reflective Thoughts:

_____
_____
_____

June
Day 6

Good morning, I hope all is well with you this lovely morning. I hope you have a fantastic, miraculous, and spectacular day today.

Reflective Thoughts:

_____
_____
_____

June
Day 7

Good morning, I hope all is well with you this lovely morning. I hope you take a moment to listen to the quietness of the morning, watch the sunrise, and hear the birds chirping today.

Reflective Thoughts:
_____
_____
_____

June
Day 8

Good morning, I hope all is well with you this lovely morning. If you ever find yourself in a position where your integrity is being challenged, I hope that you choose to display courage, fight to maintain your integrity and know that you will be rewarded in the end.

Reflective Thoughts:

_____
_____
_____

June
Day 9

Good morning, I hope all is well with you this lovely morning. I hope you encourage, lift-up, and make others laugh with joy today.

Reflective Thoughts:
_____
_____
_____

June
Day 10

Good morning, I hope all is well with you this lovely morning. I hope you have a grandiose, magnanimous, and superb day today.

Reflective Thoughts:

_____
_____
_____

June
Day 11

Good morning, I hope all is well with you this lovely morning. I hope your countenance is like the clearest sky, your words flow like the bluest sea, and your smile is bright as the Sun today.

Reflective Thoughts:

_____
_____
_____

June
Day 12

Good morning, I hope all is well with you this lovely morning. I hope that your effervescent, sparkling, and vivacious persona is on full display today.

Reflective Thoughts:
___
___
___

June
Day 13

Good morning, I hope all is well with you this lovely morning. I hope you lookout for health, interest, and wellbeing of others today.

Reflective Thoughts:
_____
_____
_____

June
Day 14

Good morning, I hope all is well with you this lovely morning. Know that your good is better, your better is best, and your best is a blessing today.

Reflective Thoughts:
_____
_____
_____

June
Day 15

Good morning, I hope all is well with you this lovely morning. I hope you are awarded a medal of goodwill, a plaque for caring, and a trophy for your sharing attitude today.

Reflective Thoughts:
___
___
___

June
Day 16

Good morning, I hope all is well with you this lovely morning. I hope your wonderful countenance brings out the good in others, encourages others to act justly, and stimulate the merriness in others today.

Reflective Thoughts:
_____
_____
_____

June
Day 17

Good morning, I hope all is well with you this lovely morning. I hope that you raise your head, lift-up your hands, and elevate your voice to give praise, honor, and thanks to God today.

Reflective Thoughts:
_____
_____
_____

June
Day 18

Good morning, I hope all is well with you this lovely morning. I hope you arose with renewed energy, renewed focus, and a renewed spirit to aid you in your accomplishments today.

Reflective Thoughts:
___
___
___

June
Day 19

Good morning, I hope all is well with you this lovely morning. I hope you are bright-eyed-and-bushy-tailed, eager, and full of energy and enthusiasm today.

Reflective Thoughts:

_____
_____
_____

June
Day 20

Good morning, I hope all is well with you this lovely morning. I hope you are full of curiosity, inquiringness, and inquisitiveness to aid you in discerning all your opportunities today.

Reflective Thoughts:
___
___
___

June
Day 21

Good morning, I hope all is well with you this lovely morning. I hope you have a day that is as cool-as-a-cucumber, as laid-back as the Caribbean, and as smooth-as-silk today.

Reflective Thoughts:
_____
_____
_____

June
Day 22

Good morning, I hope all is well with you this lovely morning. I hope that spreading joy and happiness becomes an essential, intrinsic, and an integral part of your nature today.

Reflective Thoughts:
_____
_____
_____

June
Day 23

Good morning, I hope all is well with you this lovely morning. I hope you have a phenomenal, super-sensational, and stupendous day today.

Reflective Thoughts:
___
___
___

June
Day 24

Good morning, I hope all is well with you this lovely morning. I hope you demonstrate patience, tolerance, and a but-by-the-grace-of-God-go-I attitude toward others today.

Reflective Thoughts:

_____
_____
_____

June
Day 25

Good morning, I hope all is well with you this lovely morning. I hope that you are endowed with keen-insight, sound-judgment, and razor-sharp wisdom today.

Reflective Thoughts:
_____
_____
_____

June
Day 26

Good morning, I hope all is well with you this lovely morning. I hope you arise with all the mental artillery, physical gusto, and spiritual focus to prevail over all your challenges today.

Reflective Thoughts:

_____
_____
_____

June
Day 27

Good morning, I hope all is well with you this lovely morning. I hope when you pull back the curtains, raise the shades, and open the door, happiness and good-humor rushes into your life today.

Reflective Thoughts:
_____
_____
_____

June
Day 28

Good morning, I hope all is well with you this lovely morning. I hope that with your beautiful countenance you are not disdainfully arrogant, with all the good you have do not be selfish, and whatever your position in life is do not show haughtiness today.

Reflective Thoughts:
___
___
___

June
Day 29

Good morning, I hope all is well with you this lovely morning. I hope that you're lovingly candid, illustratively frank, and tenderly evincive with all those whom you communicate with today.

Reflective Thoughts:

_____
_____
_____

June
Day 30

Good morning, I hope all is well with you this lovely morning. I hope that you are as happy as a lark, cheerful as birds early in the morning and as glorious as the sun rise today.

Reflective Thoughts:
___
___
___

July
Day 1

Good morning, I hope all is well with you this lovely morning. I hope that God's grace, loving-kindness, and mercy is bestowed upon you today.

Reflective Thoughts:
_____
_____
_____

July
Day 2

Good morning, I hope all is well with you this lovely morning. I hope that you are endowed with a chivalrous, magnanimous, and self-sacrificing spirit today.

Reflective Thoughts:
___
___
___

July
Day 3

Good morning, I hope all is well with you this lovely morning. I hope that your dynamic, electrifying, and energetic persona is on full display today.

Reflective Thoughts:

___
___
___

July
Day 4

Good morning, I hope all is well with you this lovely Independence Day morning. I hope that you have a fun-loving mythical, poetic, and fairytale day today.

Reflective Thoughts:
___
___
___

July
Day 5

Good morning, I hope all is well with you this lovely morning. I hope that you have the greatest impression, reaction, and response to everyone and everything today.

Reflective Thoughts:
_____
_____
_____

July
Day 6

Good morning, I hope all is well with you this lovely morning. I hope you have a cheery, festive, and triumphant day today.

Reflective Thoughts:
_____
_____
_____

July
Day 7

Good morning, I hope all is well with you this lovely morning. I hope that your audacious, courageous, and venturous persona is on full display today.

Reflective Thoughts:

_____
_____
_____

July
Day 8

Good morning, I hope all is well with you this lovely morning. If there is a grain of bitterness within you, replace it with pounds of joy; if there is an ounce of evil within you, replace it with a river overflowing with happiness; and if there is smidgen of hate within you, replace it with a mountain of love today.

Reflective Thoughts:

July
Day 9

Good morning, I hope all is well with you this lovely morning. I hope that your actions are not from anger, rage, or selfishness today.

Reflective Thoughts:

_____
_____
_____

July
Day 10

Good morning, I hope all is well with you this lovely morning. I hope you look with great anticipation, expectation, and excitement how God is going to work in your life today.

Reflective Thoughts:

_____
_____
_____

July
Day 11

Good morning, I hope all is well with you this lovely morning. hope you let your mind envision greatness, dream-big-dreams, and step into your {vision} this day.

Reflective Thoughts:
___
___
___

July
Day 12

Good morning, I hope all is well with you this lovely morning. I hope God grants you great favor, knowledge, and understanding in all things today.

Reflective Thoughts:
___
___
___

July
Day 13

Good morning, I hope all is well with you this lovely morning. I hope you have one of the most exciting, electrifying, and eye-popping fun-filled day today.

Reflective Thoughts:

_____
_____
_____

July
Day 14

Good morning, I hope all is well with you this lovely morning. I hope you bring cheerfulness, enjoyment, and happiness to everyone you encounter today.

Reflective Thoughts:
_____
_____
_____

July
Day 15

Good morning, I hope all is well with you this lovely morning. I hope your words bring comfort, your performance instills confidence, and your deeds bring about inspiration in others today.

Reflective Thoughts:

_____
_____
_____

July
Day 16

Good morning, I hope all is well with you this lovely morning. Be mindful that you can not control the thoughts that comes into you mind, but you can control how you respond to the thoughts that comes into your mind today.

Reflective Thoughts:

_____
_____
_____

July
Day 17

Good morning, I hope all is well with you this lovely morning. I hope that you gain prominence, rise in stature, and achieve greatness today.

Reflective Thoughts:
_____
_____
_____

July
Day 18

Good morning, I hope all is well with you this lovely morning. I hope that your commendable, esteemed, and sterling character is on full display today.

Reflective Thoughts:
_____
_____
_____

July
Day 19

Good morning, I hope all is well with you this lovely morning. Be mindful of this profound quote: "Not everything that is faced can be changed. But nothing can be changed until it is faced" today. --James Arthur Baldwin—

Reflective Thoughts:
___
___
___

July
Day 20

Good morning, I hope all is well with you this lovely morning. I hope you know that tribulation brings about perseverance; and perseverance, proven character; and proven character, hope; and hope does not disappoint, because the love of God today. NASB Roman: 5

Reflective Thoughts:

July
Day 21

Good morning, I hope all is well with you this lovely morning. I hope that your heart, soul, and mind are the benefactors of earthly, heavenly, and spiritual gifts today.

Reflective Thoughts:
_____
_____
_____

July
Day 22

Good morning, I hope all is well with you this lovely morning. I hope that you experience a state of intense happiness, take a ride on cloud-nine, and succumb to total euphoria today.

Reflective Thoughts:

_____
_____
_____

July
Day 23

Good morning, I hope all is well with you this lovely morning. I hope that you are analytical, inquisitive, and probative when seeking answers today.

Reflective Thoughts:
___
___
___

July
Day 24

Good morning, I hope all is well with you this lovely morning. I hope that you are cogitative, introspective, and thoughtful with all your decisions today.

Reflective Thoughts:
_____
_____
_____

July
Day 25

Good morning, I hope all is well with you this lovely morning. I hope that you encounter the warmest-of-hearts, the friendliest-gestures, and the greatest-of-hospitality today.

Reflective Thoughts:

_____
_____
_____

July
Day 26

Good morning, I hope all is well with you this lovely morning. I hope that you experience jumping for joy, shouting with happiness, and clapping with amusement today.

Reflective Thoughts:
___
___
___

July
Day 27

Good morning, I hope all is well with you this lovely morning. I hope your day is filled with magnificent chances, outstanding opportunities, and wonderful surprises today.

Reflective Thoughts:
_____
_____
_____

July
Day 28

Good morning, I hope all is well with you this lovely morning. I hope you are blessed with the confidence to soar like an eagle, swim like a fish, and hunt like a lion today.

Reflective Thoughts:
___
___

July
Day 29

Good morning, I hope all is well with you this lovely morning. I hope you don't hesitate to help others, because you have be helped along the way; encourage others, because you have received encouragement; and embrace others, because you have been embraced.

Reflective Thoughts:
___
___
___

July
Day 30

Good morning, I hope all is well with you this lovely morning. I hope you have a very relaxing, soothing, and therapeutic day today.

Reflective Thoughts:
___
___
___

July
Day 31

Good morning, I hope all is well with you this lovely morning. I hope that your keen insight, razor-sharp perception and penetrating discernment are on full display today.

Reflective Thoughts:
___
___
___

August
Day 1

Good morning, I hope all is well with you this lovely morning. I hope that God's grace, loving-kindness, and mercy is bestowed upon you today.

Reflective Thoughts:
___
___
___

August
Day 2

Good morning, I hope all is well with you this lovely morning. I hope you have a compassionate, giving, and sharing attitude today.

Reflective Thoughts:
___
___
___

August
Day 3

Good morning, I hope all is well with you this lovely morning. I hope that your distinguished, graceful, and honorable character is on full display today.

Reflective Thoughts:
___
___
___

August
Day 4

Good morning, I hope all is well with you this lovely morning. I hope your creative, innovative, and visionary spirit is fully active today.

Reflective Thoughts:
_____
_____
_____

August
Day 5

Good morning, I hope all is well with you this lovely morning. I hope that your effervescent, sparkling, and vivacious persona is on full display today.

Reflective Thoughts:

___
___
___

August
Day 6

Good morning, I hope all is well with you this lovely morning. I hope you are granted favor, kindness, and goodwill from all those you encounter and in all the things you do today.

Reflective Thoughts:
___
___
___

August
Day 7

Good morning, I hope all is well with you this lovely morning. I hope you act with eagerness, passion, and zeal in all that you do today.

Reflective Thoughts:

___
___
___

August
Day 8

Good morning, I hope all is well with you this lovely morning. I hope you imagine rising with a view of the most beautiful sunrise above the highest mountain, reflecting on the bluest ocean with white-sandy beaches today, because when it happens to you, you're going to say; Déjà vu.

Reflective Thoughts:

_____
_____
_____

August
Day 9

Good morning, I hope all is well with you this lovely morning. I hope your eyes are open to understanding, knowledge is placed in your mind, and wisdom placed upon your heart today.

Reflective Thoughts:

August
Day 10

Good morning, I hope all is well with you this lovely morning. I hope that your lively, spirited, and vivacious countenance is on full display today.

Reflective Thoughts:

_____
_____
_____

August
Day 11

Good morning, I hope all is well with you this lovely morning. I hope you have an exceptional, extraordinary, and phenomenal day today.

Reflective Thoughts:
_____
_____
_____

August
Day 12

Good morning, I hope all is well with you this lovely morning. I hope that your spirit of optimism is renewed, rejuvenated, and stimulated today.

Reflective Thoughts:

___
___
___

August
Day 13

Good morning, I hope all is well with you this lovely morning. I hope you show compassion, empathy, and tenderness toward others today.

Reflective Thoughts:

_____
_____
_____

August
Day 14

Good morning, I hope all is well with you this lovely morning. I hope you have an amusing, gut-busting, and laughable day today.

Reflective Thoughts:

_____
_____
_____

August
Day 15

Good morning, I hope all is well with you this lovely morning. I hope that you are willing to give back to life more that what life has given you, cherish more those who cherish you, and love more deeply than those who love you today.

Reflective Thoughts:
_____
_____
_____

August
Day 16

Good morning, I hope all is well with you this lovely morning. I hope that you are successful, triumphant, and victorious in all that you encounter today.

Reflective Thoughts:
_____
_____
_____

August
Day 17

Good morning, I hope all is well with you this lovely morning. I hope that you put on your benevolent, magnanimous, and selfless, countenance today.

Reflective Thoughts:
_____
_____
_____

August
Day 18

Good morning, I hope all is well with you this lovely morning. I hope you have an exceptionally beautiful, extraordinarily fine, and exquisitely pleasing day today.

Reflective Thoughts:
___
___
___

August
Day 19

Good morning, I hope all is well with you this lovely morning. I hope that you bestow upon others at least an ounce of your charm, joy, and love today.

Reflective Thoughts:
___
___
___

August
Day 20

Good morning, I hope all is well with you this lovely morning. I hope you have an award-winning, creative, and productive day today.

Reflective Thoughts:
_____
_____
_____

August
Day 21

Good morning, I hope all is well with you this lovely morning. I hope your day is filled with great opportunities, significant personal development, and outstanding life changing experiences today.

Reflective Thoughts:
___
___
___

August
Day 22

Good morning, I hope all is well with you this lovely morning. I hope that you paint a meaningful reflective picture with your thoughts, that your words flow as poetry, and your gestures impart laughter to everyone you encounter today.

Reflective Thoughts:

_____
_____
_____

August
Day 23

Good morning, I hope all is well with you this lovely morning. I hope your mind, body and soul are re-energized, rejuvenated, and reinvigorated today.

Reflective Thoughts:
_____
_____
_____

August
Day 24

Good morning, I hope all is well with you this lovely morning. I hope that you elevate, exalt, and uplift others today.

Reflective Thoughts:
___
___
___

August
Day 25

Good morning, I hope all is well with you this lovely morning. I hope you have an awesome, majestic, and smashing day today.

Reflective Thoughts:
_____
_____
_____

August
Day 26

Good morning, I hope all is well with you this lovely morning. I hope you are met with authentic, honest-to-goodness, and genuine receptiveness from all those you encounter today.

Reflective Thoughts:
_____
_____
_____

August
Day 27

Good morning, I hope all is well with you this lovely morning. I hope you are bedecked in your first-rate awesomeness, brilliance, and dignity today.

Reflective Thoughts:
_____
_____
_____

August
Day 28

Good morning, I hope all is well with you this lovely morning. I hope that you are steadfast in keeping the faith, maintaining your optimism, and firm in your beliefs today.

Reflective Thoughts:
___
___
___

August
Day 29

Good morning, I hope all is well with you this lovely morning. I hope you find these quotes stimulating to your thought process today:

- "Chance favors the prepared mind." ~By Louis Pasteur~
- Presenting a reason for your action/non-action is better than giving an excuse for your action/non-action. Making an "Effort" provides a reason. ~My Reflective Thought~
- "A friend's eye is a good mirror" – [A real friend will tell you the truth.] ~Irish Proverb~

Reflective Thoughts:
___
___
___

August
Day 30

Good morning, I hope all is well with you this lovely morning. I hope that your faith in your visions are amplified, enhanced, and reinforced by the wonderful people and things you encounter today.

Reflective Thoughts:

_____
_____
_____

August
Day 31

Good morning, I hope all is well with you this lovely morning. I hope that even on a cloudy day you have sunshine on your heart, a clear-blue-sky in your eyes, and a warm-summer-breeze on your mind today.

Reflective Thoughts:

___
___
___

September
Day 1

Good morning, I hope all is well with you this lovely morning. I hope that God's grace, loving-kindness, and mercy is bestowed upon you today.

Reflective Thoughts:

_____
_____
_____

September
Day 2

Good morning, I hope all is well with you this lovely morning. I hope that you are blessed with determination, resourcefulness, and resiliency to deal skillfully and promptly with all the obstacles you face today.

Reflective Thoughts:

_____
_____
_____

September
Day 3

Good morning, I hope all is well with you this lovely morning. I hope that you don't hesitant to give an appreciative handshake, a grateful smile, and a thankful hug to those whom it's due today.

Reflective Thoughts:

___
___
___

September
Day 4

Good morning, I hope all is well with you this lovely morning. I hope that all you do is extremely valuable, very constructive, and exceedingly rewarding today.

Reflective Thoughts:
___
___
___

September
Day 5

Good morning, I hope all is well with you this lovely morning. I hope that you can find contentment, fulfillment, and serenity in all that you do today.

Reflective Thoughts:

_____
_____
_____

September
Day 6

Good morning, I hope all is well with you this lovely morning. I hope the look in your eyes, the smile on your face, and the words from your mouth brings joy to all those you encounter today.

Reflective Thoughts:
___
___
___

September
Day 7

Good morning, I hope all is well with you this lovely morning. I hope that you're courageous, steadfast, and tireless effort is on full display in pursuing your vision today.

Reflective Thoughts:

_____
_____
_____

September
Day 8

Good morning, I hope all is well with you this lovely morning. I hope that you are adorned with your thrilling flair, rip-roaring pizazz, and eye-popping style today.

Reflective Thoughts:
___
___
___

September
Day 9

Good morning, I hope all is well with you this lovely morning. I hope you have a delightful, festive, and joyous day today.

Reflective Thoughts:

_____
_____
_____

September
Day 10

Good morning, I hope all is well with you this lovely morning. I hope you have a very blooming, prosperous, and successful day today.

Reflective Thoughts:
___
___
___

September
Day 11

Good morning, I hope all is well with you this lovely morning. I hope you know that God made you an extraordinary, distinctive, and special person. Therefore, by giving up, you would never realize God's full plan for you today and the next day.

Reflective Thoughts:
_____
_____
_____

September
Day 12

Good morning, I hope all is well with you this lovely morning. I hope that all your gifts, ingenuity, and talents are on full display today.

Reflective Thoughts:
_____
_____
_____

September
Day 13

Good morning, I hope all is well with you this lovely morning.   I hope that your affable, gracious, and suave persona is exhibited today.

Reflective Thoughts:

_____
_____
_____

September
Day 14

Good morning, I hope all is well with you this lovely morning. I hope you impart fervency, kindness, and warmth to everyone you encounter today.

Reflective Thoughts:

September
Day 15

Good morning, I hope all is well with you this lovely morning. I hope you become rich with an attitude of giving, protecting and serving others today.

Reflective Thoughts:
___
___
___

September
Day 16

Good morning, I hope all is well with you this lovely morning. I hope you look with great anticipation, expectation, and hopefulness the wonderful things God is going to do in your life today.

Reflective Thoughts:

September
Day 17

Good morning, I hope all is well with you this lovely morning. I hope you know that you are a blessing, a gift, and a testimonial of God everyday, especially today.

Reflective Thoughts:

_____
_____
_____

September
Day 18

Good morning, I hope all is well with you this lovely morning. I hope you're able to demonstrate longanimity, patient-endurance, and self-control in all the challenges you encounter today.

Reflective Thoughts:
___
___
___

September
Day 19

Good morning, I hope all is well with you this lovely morning. I hope your creativity, ingenuity, and imagination is firing on all cylinders today.

Reflective Thoughts:
_____
_____
_____

September
Day 20

Good morning, I hope all is well with you this lovely morning. I hope you maintain a healthy, joyous, and sprightly frame-of-mind today.

Reflective Thoughts:
_____
_____
_____

September
Day 21

Good morning, I hope all is well with you this lovely morning. I hope you have a mellow, relaxing, and soothing day today.

Reflective Thoughts:

_____
_____
_____

September
Day 22

Good morning, I hope all is well with you this lovely morning. Although your mind at times may want to focus on the past, work to stay-in-the-moment, be forward-looking and forward-thinking today.

Reflective Thoughts:

_____

_____

_____

September
Day 23

Good morning, I hope all is well with you this lovely morning. I hope your charisma, glamour, and magnetism is on full display today.

Reflective Thoughts:
___
___
___

September
Day 24

Good morning, I hope all is well with you this lovely morning. I hope you have a delightful, fascinating, and ravishing day today.

Reflective Thoughts:
_____
_____
_____

September
Day 25

Good morning, I hope all is well with you this lovely morning. I hope you have an accommodating, giving, and sharing spirit today.

Reflective Thoughts:

_____
_____
_____

September
Day 26

Good morning, I hope all is well with you this lovely morning. I hope that your charismatic, lodestone, and magnetic qualities brings out the best in the people you encounter today.

Reflective Thoughts:

_____
_____
_____

September
Day 27

Good morning, I hope all is well with you this lovely morning. I hope that you display courageousness, great fortitude, and perseverance while facing all your challenges today.

Reflective Thoughts:

_____

_____

_____

September
Day 28

Good morning, I hope all is well with you this lovely morning. I hope that your charisma, flamboyant-spirit, and get-up-and-go attitude is on full display today.

Reflective Thoughts:
___
___
___

September
Day 29

Good morning, I hope all is well with you this lovely morning. I hope that you are very meticulous about those wonderfully deliberate, intentional, and purposeful things you do today.

Reflective Thoughts:

_____
_____
_____

September
Day 30

Good morning, I hope all is well with you this lovely morning. I hope that your persona expresses appreciation, gratefulness, and thankfulness for who you are and all that you have today.

Reflective Thoughts:
_____
_____
_____

October
Day 1

Good morning, I hope all is well with you this lovely morning. I hope that God's grace, loving-kindness, and mercy is bestowed upon you today.

Reflective Thoughts:

_____
_____
_____

October
Day 2

Good morning, I hope all is well with you this lovely morning. I hope that your effervescent, illuminating, and scintillating personality is on full display today.

Reflective Thoughts:
___
___
___

October
Day 3

Good morning, I hope all is well with you this lovely morning. I hope that you elevate, uplift, and raise-the-spirit of others today.

Reflective Thoughts:
___
___
___

October
Day 4

Good morning, I hope all is well with you this lovely morning. I hope that your competent, proficient, and skillful talents are on full display today.

Reflective Thoughts:

_____

_____

_____

October
Day 5

Good morning, I hope all is well with you this lovely morning. I hope you have a dynamic, wonderful-life-changing, and an unforgettable day today.

Reflective Thoughts:

_____
_____
_____

October
Day 6

Good morning, I hope all is well with you this lovely morning. I hope that you have an effective, impactful, and impressive day today.

Reflective Thoughts:

October
Day 7

Good morning, I hope all is well with you this lovely morning. I hope that you are filled with gladness, laughter, and rejoicing today.

Reflective Thoughts:

_____
_____
_____

October
Day 8

Good morning, I hope all is well with you this lovely morning. I hope you are willing to challenge the world by stirring-up the status quo, upsetting the proverbial apple cart, and being an agitator of life for the good today.

Reflective Thoughts:

October
Day 9

Good morning, I hope all is well with you this lovely morning. I hope you have an electrifying, eye-popping, and groovy day today.

Reflective Thoughts:
___
___
___

October
Day 10

Good morning, I hope all is well with you this lovely morning. I hope that your masterful, proficient, and superlative skills are on full display today.

Reflective Thoughts:

_____
_____
_____

October
Day 11

Good morning, I hope all is well with you this lovely morning. I hope that your life is filled with brilliance, majesty, and splendor today.

Reflective Thoughts:

_____

_____

_____

October
Day 12

Good morning, I hope all is well with you this lovely morning. I hope that you don't hesitate to give admiration, homage, and praise to others today.

Reflective Thoughts:
_____
_____
_____

October
Day 13

Good morning, I hope all is well with you this lovely morning. I hope that you wear your effervescent, sparkling, and vivacious persona today.

Reflective Thoughts:

_____
_____
_____

October
Day 14

Good morning, I hope all is well with you this lovely morning. I hope that you envision, imagine, and vicariously visit your favorite places throughout the world today.

Reflective Thoughts:

October
Day 15

Good morning, I hope all is well with you this lovely morning. I hope for your breakfast; your cup overflows with joy, your bowl is full of happiness, and your plate is stacked with glory today.

Reflective Thoughts:

_____
_____
_____

October
Day 16

Good morning, I hope all is well with you this lovely morning. I hope that you show your generous cacophonous, rambunctious, and raucous, disposition in order to make things happen for others today.

Reflective Thoughts:

October
Day 17

Good morning, I hope all is well with you this lovely morning. I hope that your inherent, intrinsic, and natural wonderful qualities are on full display today.

Reflective Thoughts:

_____
_____
_____

October
Day 18

Good morning, I hope all is well with you this lovely morning. I hope that you show your big-hearted, charitable, and humanitarian disposition today.

Reflective Thoughts:
___
___
___

October
Day 19

Good morning, I hope all is well with you this lovely morning. I hope your day is filled with amusement, charm, and pleasantries today.

Reflective Thoughts:

_____
_____
_____

October
Day 20

Good morning, I hope all is well with you this lovely morning. I hope you have a calm, carefree, and happy-go-lucky day today.

Reflective Thoughts:
___
___
___

October
Day 21

Good morning, I hope all is well with you this lovely morning. I hope that you reflect and remain firm, steadfast, and true-blue to your vision each day, especially today.

Reflective Thoughts:
___

October
Day 22

Good morning, I hope all is well with you this lovely morning. I hope you uplift rather than teardown, inspire rather than denigrate, and embrace rather than shun your friends and foes alike today.

Reflective Thoughts:

_____
_____
_____

October
Day 23

Good morning, I hope all is well with you this lovely morning. I hope your gleaming, radiant, and resplendent persona is on full display today.

Reflective Thoughts:
___
___
___

October
Day 24

Good morning, I hope all is well with you this lovely morning. I hope you give your very best, at whatever you're doing, at the very moment you're doing it, today.

Reflective Thoughts:

_____
_____
_____

October
Day 25

Good morning, I hope all is well with you this lovely morning. I hope you are full-of-life, high-spirited, and peppy today.

Reflective Thoughts:

_____
_____
_____

October
Day 26

Good morning, I hope all is well with you this lovely morning. I hope that your adorable, delightful, and suave persona is exhibited today.

Reflective Thoughts:

_____
_____
_____

October
Day 27

Good morning, I hope all is well with you this lovely morning. I hope that your bewitching, enchanting, and enthralling smile uplifts everyone you encounter today.

Reflective Thoughts:

_____
_____
_____

October
Day 28

Good morning, I hope all is well with you this lovely morning. I hope that you are certain of yourself today, as the river does flows, the sun does shines, and the wind does blows.

Reflective Thoughts:

_____
_____
_____

October
Day 29

Good morning, I hope all is well with you this lovely morning. I hope the weather forecast for you will be; a sunny-personality, a blue-sky-smile, and a pleasantly balmy-disposition today.

Reflective Thoughts:
_____
_____
_____

October
Day 30

Good morning, I hope all is well with you this lovely morning. I hope that you maintain a hopeful, optimistic, and positive view about your future today.

Reflective Thoughts:
___
___
___

October
Day 31

Good morning, I hope all is well with you this lovely morning. I hope that your artistic, ingenious, and sagacious frame-of-mind is fully active today.

Reflective Thoughts:

_____
_____
_____

November
Day 1

Good morning, I hope all is well with you this lovely morning. I hope that God's grace, loving-kindness, and mercy is bestowed upon you today.

Reflective Thoughts:
___
___
___

November
Day 2

Good morning, I hope all is well with you this lovely morning. Your strength is in your ability to adapt to circumstances while simultaneously moving forward, your courage is in your willingness to look out for the interest of others, and your get-up-and-go attitude is from your determination to live into your vision until it attains itself today and forever.

Reflective Thoughts:

_____
_____
_____

November
Day 3

Good morning, I hope all is well with you this lovely morning. I hope that you are filled with great joy, big-smiles, and wonderful surprises today.

Reflective Thoughts:

_____
_____
_____

November
Day 4

Good morning, I hope all is well with you this lovely morning. I hope that you know you are the child of an immutable, omnipotent, and omnipresent awesome God that looks after you everyday, especially today.

Reflective Thoughts:

_____
_____
_____

November
Day 5

Good morning, I hope all is well with you this lovely morning. I hope that you are creative, enterprising, and innovative today.

Reflective Thoughts:

_____
_____
_____

November
Day 6

Good morning, I hope all is well with you this lovely morning. I hope that you shower all those you encounter with your benevolent, humanitarian, and kind-hearted spirit today.

Reflective Thoughts:

_____
_____
_____

November
Day 7

Good morning, I hope all is well with you this lovely morning. I hope that you're able to summons all your fortitude, moxie, and strength, to take on all challenges you encounter today.

Reflective Thoughts:

_____
_____
_____

November
Day 8

Good morning, I hope all is well with you this lovely morning. If you can hear, see, or feel one or more of these early morning 'quiet-sounds' of life:

- The sound of a train whistle in a distance,
- The sound of waves brushing upon the land, and
- A breeze ruffling the tree leaves,

Take a moment to take it in today.

Reflective Thoughts:
_____
_____
_____

November
Day 9

Good morning, I hope all is well with you this lovely morning. I hope your countenance is a ray-of-hope, spirit-uplifting, and an excitement to the soul today.

Reflective Thoughts:
_____
_____
_____

November
Day 10

Good morning, I hope all is well with you this lovely morning. I hope that you demonstrate forbearance, patient-endurance, and self-control in managing obstacles you may encounter today.

Reflective Thoughts:

November
Day 11

Good morning, I hope all is well with you this lovely morning. I hope you have a colorful, picturesque, and quaint day today.

Reflective Thoughts:

November
Day 12

Good morning, I hope all is well with you this lovely morning. I hope you display a festive, gleeful, and upbeat attitude today.

Reflective Thoughts:
_____
_____
_____

November
Day 13

Good morning, I hope all is well with you this lovely morning. I hope that your wonderful distinguished, peculiar, and unique personality shines through today.

Reflective Thoughts:
_____
_____
_____

November
Day 14

Good morning, I hope all is well with you this lovely morning. I hope that you show generosity, goodwill, and tolerance to all the people you encounter today.

Reflective Thoughts:

___
___
___

November
Day 15

Good morning, I hope all is well with you this lovely morning. I hope that when facing any challenges or obstacles, you maintain your pristine, untarnished, and wholesome reputation today.

Reflective Thoughts:

_____
_____
_____

November
Day 16

Good morning, I hope all is well with you this lovely morning. I hope that you employ great knowledge, practical wisdom, and sound understanding in all situations you encounter today.

Reflective Thoughts:

_____
_____
_____

November
Day 17

Good morning, I hope all is well with you this lovely morning. I hope that the welcoming look in your eyes, the smile on your face, and the sound of your voice brings joy to others today.

Reflective Thoughts:

_____
_____
_____

November
Day 18

Good morning, I hope all is well with you this lovely morning. I hope you have a prosperous, rewarding, and triumphant day today.

Reflective Thoughts:
_____
_____
_____

November
Day 19

Good morning, I hope all is well with you this lovely morning. I hope you promote happiness, swap a smile, and trade some cheer today.

Reflective Thoughts:
_____
_____
_____

November
Day 20

Good morning, I hope all is well with you this lovely morning. I hope that you are operating with clear eyes, a pure heart, and an impeccable mind today.

Reflective Thoughts:

_____
_____
_____

November
Day 21

Good morning, I hope all is well with you this lovely morning. I hope you bring forth your forward-looking, open-minded, and revolutionary ideas today.

Reflective Thoughts:

_____
_____
_____

November
Day 22

Good morning, I hope all is well with you this lovely morning. I hope you pursue that, which will provide satisfaction to your conscious, gratification to your soul, and fulfillment to your socially-engaging-self today.

Reflective Thoughts:

_____
_____
_____

November
Day 23

Good morning, I hope all is well with you this lovely morning. I hope your mind is saturated with the glorious-of-thoughts, the praising-of-God, and the cherishing-of-human-kind today.

Reflective Thoughts:

_____
_____
_____

November
Day 24

Good morning, I hope all is well with you this lovely morning. I hope that your heart is filled with generosity, goodwill, and graciousness today.

Reflective Thoughts:
_____
_____
_____

November
Day 25

Good morning, I hope all is well with you this lovely morning. I hope that your adaptability, discernment, and savoir-faire qualities are fully recognized today.

Reflective Thoughts:
___
___
___

November
Day 26

Good morning, I hope all is well with you this lovely morning. I hope that you dazzle the world with your dashing smile, gracious charm, and chichi style today.

Reflective Thoughts:

_____
_____
_____

November
Day 27

Good morning, I hope all is well with you this lovely morning. I hope you have an easy-going, straightforward, and smooth day today.

Reflective Thoughts:
_____
_____
_____

November
Day 28

Good morning, I hope all is well with you this lovely morning. I hope you spread your kindness as wide as the sea, as broad as the sky, and as vast as the earth today.

Reflective Thoughts:
_____
_____
_____

November
Day 29

Good morning, I hope all is well with you this lovely morning. I hope you have pep-in-your-step, oomph-in-your-stride, and vitality-in-your-reality today.

Reflective Thoughts:
___
___
___

November
Day 30

Good morning, I hope all is well with you this lovely morning. I hope you do all things efficiently, proficiently, and sufficiently today.

Reflective Thoughts:
___
___
___

December
Day 1

Good morning, I hope all is well with you this lovely morning. I hope that God's grace, loving-kindness, and mercy is bestowed upon you today.

Reflective Thoughts:
_____
_____
_____

December
Day 2

Good morning, I hope all is well with you this lovely morning. I hope that your dynamic, effervescent, and energetic persona is on full display today.

Reflective Thoughts:

___
___
___

December
Day 3

Good morning, I hope all is well with you this lovely morning. I hope that you exemplify gentleness, kindness, and tenderness toward others today.

Reflective Thoughts:
_____
_____
_____

December
Day 4

Good morning, I hope all is well with you this lovely morning. I hope that you demonstrate flexibility, resiliency, and vigor as you pursue your goals and visions today.

Reflective Thoughts:
_____
_____
_____

December
Day 5

Good morning, I hope all is well with you this lovely morning. I hope that you remain focused on your vision, stay-in-the conversation about your vision, and step-into your vision until it attains itself each day.

Reflective Thoughts:
_____
_____
_____

December
Day 6

Good morning, I hope all is well with you this lovely morning. I hope you have an incalculable, incredible, and an immeasurable super-fantastic day today.

Reflective Thoughts:
_____
_____
_____

December
Day 7

Good morning, I hope all is well with you this lovely morning. I hope you still-a-moment to let your mind meditate, ponder, and reflect on all the things to be thankful for today.

Reflective Thoughts:
_____
_____
_____

December
Day 8

Good morning, I hope all is well with you this lovely morning. I hope you assign yourself a realistic achievable mission, give yourself a standing ovation upon its achievement, and treat yourself to something nice for that accomplishment today.

Reflective Thoughts:
___
___
___

December
Day 9

Good morning, I hope all is well with you this lovely morning. I hope you're able to summons absolute knowledge, understanding, and wisdom to address all your concerns and interests today.

Reflective Thoughts:
_____
_____
_____

December
Day 10

Good morning, I hope all is well with you this lovely morning. I hope you are full of electrifying, dynamic, and high-powered-productive energy today.

Reflective Thoughts:
___
___
___

December
Day 11

Good morning, I hope all is well with you this lovely morning. I hope you exude uninhibited-enthusiasm, extreme-joy, and abundance-of-happiness today.

Reflective Thoughts:
___
___
___

December
Day 12

Good morning, I hope all is well with you this lovely morning. I hope God grants you all your needs, wants, and desires today.

Reflective Thoughts:
_____
_____
_____

December
Day 13

Good morning, I hope all is well with you this lovely morning. I hope that your beautiful, elegant, and electrifying disposition is on full display today.

Reflective Thoughts:
_____
_____
_____

December
Day 14

Good morning, I hope all is well with you this lovely morning. I hope that you approach this Holiday season remembering those who are homeless, hungry, and destitute, especially the children today.

Reflective Thoughts:

_____
_____
_____

December
Day 15

Good morning, I hope all is well with you this lovely morning. When you know you ought to be doing something, just do it; don't put off what you can do today until tomorrow, because tomorrow will have its own challenges; and pat yourself on the back for making it happen today.

Reflective Thoughts:
___
___
___

December
Day 16

Good morning, I hope all is well with you this lovely morning. I hope you are rejuvenated with robust, vigorous, and zealous energy today.

Reflective Thoughts:
_____
_____
_____

December
Day 17

Good morning, I hope all is well with you this lovely morning. I hope you let your ears hear, your eyes see, your heart feel, and your mind understand that the greatest start of this day is when you arose this morning. You can choose to be consumed be negativity or positivity. Your choice.

Reflective Thoughts:

_____
_____
_____

December
Day 18

Good morning, I hope all is well with you this lovely morning. I hope you are super-sensational, super-terrific, and topnotch at everything you do today.

Reflective Thoughts:
___
___
___

December
Day 19

Good morning, I hope all is well with you this lovely morning. I hope you remember God gave you a great mind to gain as much knowledge as you seek, to understand as much as you desire, and to imagine anything without limitation each day, especially today.

Reflective Thoughts:
_____
_____
_____

December
Day 20

Good morning, I hope all is well with you this lovely morning. I hope that the meditation of your heart and the words from your mouth brings harmony, serenity, and tranquility to everyone you encounter today.

Reflective Thoughts:
_____
_____
_____

December
Day 21

G ood morning, I hope all is well with you this lovely morning. I hope your courageousness, charisma, and flamboyant-spirit is on full display today.

Reflective Thoughts:
_____
_____
_____

December
Day 22

Good morning, I hope all is well with you this lovely morning. I hope you take the time to send someone an encouraging word, get together for a positive chat even if it's for just a minute, and go out your way to say something that's honest and nice about that person to someone else today.

Reflective Thoughts:
___
___
___

Authors Prerogative: Happy Birthday to my late Ma-Dear and in memorial to all the other Mothers that has passed on.

December
Day 23

Good morning, I hope all is well with you this lovely morning. I hope you exhibit your A-okay, exquisite, and impeccable qualities today.

Reflective Thoughts:
_____
_____
_____

December
Day 24

Good morning, I hope all is well with you this lovely morning. I hope your day is as beautiful as the sun rising, as delightful as birds chirping and as smooth as the sound of the ocean waves today.

Reflective Thoughts:
_____
_____
_____

December
Day 25

Good morning, I hope all is well with you this lovely Christ's Birthday morning. I hope you are rewarded with good health, great success, and lasting financial security today.

Reflective Thoughts:
_____
_____
_____

December
Day 26

Good morning, I hope all is well with you this lovely morning. I hope you have a willingness to share your blessings, good-fortune, and goodness with those in need that you encounter today.

Reflective Thoughts:

_____
_____
_____

December
Day 27

Good morning, I hope all is well with you this lovely morning. I hope people are wonderfully courteous, pleasantly kind, and extremely gracious to you today.

Reflective Thoughts:
___
___
___

December
Day 28

Good morning, I hope all is well with you this lovely morning. I hope that you have an assertive, optimistic, and upbeat attitude today.

Reflective Thoughts:

_____
_____
_____

December
Day 29

Good morning, I hope all is well with you this lovely morning. I hope you find a proverb, a scripture, or a philosophical creed, and write it on the tablet of your heart, recite it often, and work to live your life by it everyday.

Reflective Thoughts:
_____
_____
_____

December
Day 30

Good morning, I hope all is well with you this lovely morning. I hope that you display your engrossing, gripping, and riveting smile today.

Reflective Thoughts:

_____
_____
_____

December
Day 31

Good morning, I hope all is well with you this lovely morning. I hope that your thirst for knowledge is as deep as the ocean, as high as the mountain and as wide as the sea today.

Reflective Thoughts:
_____
_____

Made in the USA
Lexington, KY
17 September 2017